The Search

The Search

by Jennifer Langer

www.victorinapress.com

Typesetting and Layout: Jorge Vasquez
Cover design ©: Clarrie-Anne Cooper
Cover artwork : Irena Corsini
British Library Cataloguing in Publication Data
A catalogue record for this book is available from the
British Library.
ISBN: 978-1-8380360-9-6

Typeset in 12pt Garamond
Printed and bound in Great Britain by 4edge ltd.

Contents

For Stanley, Timothy and Jeremy

'There are things like reflecting pools, and images, an infinite reference from one to the other, but no longer a source, a spring. There is no longer any simple origin.'
- Jacques Derrida

Acknowledgements

I express my sincere gratitude to Amanda Huggins, poet and short story writer, who gave of her time in providing me with much valued constructive feedback on the collection.

My thanks and appreciation are due to the members of the poets' collective founded by Beata Duncan and now led by her son, poet Stephen Duncan. At our gatherings they generously provided helpful critique on some of the poems. In particular, I would like to thank poet Mary Woodward, for her comments and encouragement.

Many thanks to Irena Corsini for her wonderful 'Collage Painting'.

A special thank you to the publisher, Consuelo Rivera-Fuentes, and to her team for all their support.

Where Do You Really Come From?

she with her straight blonde hair and blue eyes
me with my wavy dark hair and brown eyes
one sunny afternoon on a Surrey terrace
we sat facing the tall trees and upwards sloping lawn
she asked me where I came from
I was stunned for a moment
'I'm English' I said. 'I was born here'
She replied 'Yes I know, but where do you really come from?'
I wanted to shout out 'I am as English as you'
yet I succumbed, revealed my parents' background
'My parents were from Germany' I said
she looked puzzled. I did not look German either
I left her guessing for a moment
Then I added 'They escaped from the Nazis'
finally she understood.
will there ever come a time when I will be English?

The Search

I Could Have Been

Dedicated to Freddie, murdered by the Nazis in 1942 at the age of three

I could have run along silent streets sheltered by fluttering trees
past gloomy church spires rising to the sky
I would not have entered to genuflect on my knees
I could have been a child of Uruguay

skipping past the café sounds of scratched songs soaring
into the sun-filled desert of the naked square
the shaking mirage of the hidden house imploring
this is a house of trauma but of that I am unaware

I could have knelt on a wooden window seat
staring at the confused snow rushing and fleeing
cousin Freddie would have come searching for me
I could have been a child of Germany
scampering along the dark corridor
smothering him with kisses, more and more

The Search

In Her Shoes

Calais Fréthun station lies heavy with silence
marooned in the night outside time
steel walls, steel ceiling sting with cold
watching figures wait in the shadows

she hugs her rucksack like a baby
the Eritrean woman is on the prowl
CCTV is rolling, police eyes darting
I could have been her, she me

the Eurostar's sliding doors rush open
the warm coffeed carriage sucks me in
the doors snap shut like a crocodile's mouth
you me rejected, me you trudge back to Camp

the train races against the night of mist
and the memory of my guilt

The Search

A Room in Austria

eyes riveted on the huge wooden cross
reflected endlessly in the mirror
emaciated man outstretched, head drooping
a skinny dark-haired girl
shrieks
refuses to scramble onto the country bed
refuses to sleep below the tortured man
on the wall of the Austrian village room
her parents cajole and reason
finally cover Jesus with a towel.

The Search

Limbo, Limbus

you lift and drag your feet
out of the squelching mud
the rain issues from dark skies
creates a patter on flimsy tents
the downpour a drumbeat on plastic roofs
cars up on the autoroute
flash past in a venomous hiss of rain

do you ever sing now?
the songs of your Syrian childhood?
remember the ecstasy of the rain rhythm
on the tired palm fronds
you sing the songs so low here

never did the air smell so dank
cold seeps into your veins
gets inside your bones
salt wind blows in from the Channel
sand gusts in from the wide beaches

you survive on hope
the tentacles of obsession cling to you
nights of climbing the wire like spiders
to creep into chilling steel caverns
over and under sealed silver trains
to reach that isle of dreams

Exiled Writers Ink was at the Calais migrant camp in October 2015. UK exiled writers from Syria, Afghanistan, Eritrea and Somalia ran live literature and workshop sessions there.

The Search

Language of my Homeland

Hoppe, hoppe, Reiter
Wenn er fällt, dann schreit er
Fällt er in den Graben
Fressen ihn die Raben
Fällt er in den Sumpf
Macht der Reiter plumps!

bounce, bounce, bounce, bounce
shrill sounds of excitement
till the magical drop down
between my mother's knees
almost to the floor
but not quite
hugged tight
Hoppe, hoppe reite
a nursery rhyme sung to German children
picture books from Germany
images of girls, red-cheeked
pale hair plaited
forests of fir trees
Christmas trees
O Tannenbaum, O Tannenbaum
Wie grün sind deine Blätter

my parents' secret conversations
their problems and anxieties
still no reply from the Red Cross Tracing Service
will their families be traced
now or ever?
to me it was wall-to-wall German
the language seeped in insidiously, naturally

Naturlisch!
familiar as sauerkraut and sausages
the language of my parents, of their parents and of theirs

Tegel Airport, Berlin

travel by sleek, silent train into town
suddenly the familiar language intrudes
the language of home
my roots, and yet
I feel a shudder of revulsion

they are all staring at us
dark-haired, exotic
the remnants returned.
In the East, cobbled streets
dusty bookshop windows
packed with glossy tomes:
The Lost Jews, Vanished Jews of Germany
clearly an endangered species
religious men
black-hatted, white-bearded
gaze out from the covers

I'm bursting to sing and shout out
'It wasn't like that, I know, my mother told me'
she was a Berliner
partook of *kuchen* and *schlacksahne* in the Kudam cafes
went shopping at KaDeWe
picnicked by the Wannsee
played tennis at the sports club
no resemblance to the Teutonic reconstruction
Naturlisch!

Herero Anguish

see how the antelope and giraffe sniff around it
see how it glints rhythmically under the singing sun
with reluctance the rust-red soil releases it
the golden ball of brass nestles cold in my hand

misplaced antique relic
of German South West Africa
1915, mules and horses panted desperately
loaded with carved furniture homeward bound
the suffering earth the brass handle's burial ground

the haunted air screams with Herero anguish
the echoes of grand evenings of dinners and balls
the shattering of crystal chandeliers
the splintering of mahogany chests
the cracking of fine Meissen
now, portraits of the Kaiser and Kaiserin are fading

*Herero: African tribe oppressed and driven off their lands after tremendous battles with
the Germans. The genocide of the Herero people occurred in German South West Africa
between 1904 and 1908.*

13

The Search

Carnival Float

I strain to hear the dancing violins and accordions
the riotous rhythm of the German music
the laughter of the handsome young men
bow-tied, leather-jacketed, knickerbockered, suited
they recline on bunk beds on the carnival float
on the banner they wrote "Our Thanks to Britain"

many times I have stared at the old photo
at my father's face smiling and relaxed
they, not the drowned; they the saved
they, the chosen for rescue
in Vienna and Berlin.
later the laughter would fade

young men asleep in rows in wooden huts
marooned in mud in Sandwich, Kent
the moody moon hides behind the frenzied clouds.
In the winter woods the owl performs
streaks of black and gothic night
slide stealthily under the flimsy doors

with a rush of wings
the black eagle flies in
its dark shadow hovers
bringing deathland for hours
the past hunts down the men nocturnally
the wounds stitched closed diurnally
insistently clawed at and peeled open
the foetal men murmur, shriek and scream

and there were those at Buchenwald
who were electrocuted
who were beaten to death
who fell ill and were lost
who were forced to stand the entire night on the parade ground
who disappeared into bunkers and were not seen again
and there were those who were executed.
my father was a prisoner there

Swakopmund

the sun burnt red, it was certain to explode
your hazy domes and shivering towers lured me
sea scents drifting across the desert drew me
distant Bavarian town you fooled me

I dreamt and rose in a *pension*
under the mournful eyes of stuffed elephants' heads
in the dining room waiters flicked white tablecloths
ready for pork schnitzel, dumplings and bratwurst

men bowed low, kissed women's glittering hands
a dirndled girl with fair-haired plaits watched,
the carved map of Deutsch-Südwestafrika presided
the cuckoo clock had stopped

in Swakopmund the buzz of German threatened me
the Nazi paraphernalia scared me
the ghosts of the past tailed me
a fish out of water, I drowned in my own breath

I fled from that town on the Skeleton Coast
alone, back bent under the weight of the sky
the darkness thick as treacle
the sand billowing with the wind

and the spirits of the dead sighed
I heard the wild moan, the echo
the moon watched over the desert bones

*Swakopmund is in Namibia which was the colony of German South West Africa
from 1884 to 1915.*

The Search

No-Go Zone

the scene is set
mother and daughter are snug in Cosmo
its glossy red Gaggia hissing as usual

it's like gazing into the glare of the sun
you can't stare at it too long
broaching the subject, really it's a no-go zone
my mother fled, crossing the North Sea
at least I think she did, she must have
I heard mention that the Nazis
stole her trunks at the Hook of Holland
the daughter will write in her mother's voice
I warn you though, it may not be quite right

such a large trunk lined with striped paper
I sift through the photos, pause and gaze
me on the beach with Hildegard
I remember it was so cold, so gusty
running with the North Sea wind
shrieking like a crazed horse
I remember those hockey games in the snow
barefoot, my toes numb, my cheeks on fire
I cram in all my clothes, silk, wool, linen, tweed
I remember the dressmaker always came
those fittings, standing so still, so long
I squeeze in an English dictionary, grammar books
English was my best subject
I close the trunk of memory

the North Sea is grey and rough
Mutti and Vati are pacing the Berlin flat

their nerves shattering like shards of glass
Haman strides the land once more

the wind carries cold that slices knife-sharp
in a frenzy it scoops up my thoughts
I watch Europe float away
vanish as if it had never been

Cosmo was a café-restaurant on the Finchley Road in Swiss Cottage, London where German-speaking Jewish refugees often gathered. It was established in the 1930s by a refugee from Germany.

Haman, who appears in the Book of Esther in the Old Testament, was principal minister to King Ahasuerus who was married to Queen Esther. Haman plotted to kill her and all the Jews of the Persian Empire.

Unmasked

huge finger shadow on the wall
a long arm pointing
he runs between the brilliant light
the spotlight dazzles
he flits between brightness and darkness
a rehearsal of Oedipus
outside, the cool air of a Bologna night
his face is a smiling mask
weeping man whose tears are buried deep
Tehran sleeps within him
he is the snow of the Alborz Mountains
he is the water bubbling over the rocks
he is the fresh green of Nowruz leaves
he wears the mask of tragedy
he suffers the eternal torture of memory
he can never return
his scream bounces off the ancient city walls
the curtains swish closed

The Search

Racer

out of the haze of the Wagnerian forest
a dusty black motorbike rushes
the rider grips the handlebars tightly
his face set hard as steel
he's a knight in battle
encased in his armour of black leather
he swerves and sways deep into the bends

Viennese waltzer on wheels
he's lawless on his Rudge
number 26,
hell-bent on speed
hell-bent on winning
the mist captures him once more
my father's a ghost rider

the knock on the door at dawn
as the winter sun rose over Breslau
over the frosted rooftops
they took my father away
that was the end of the road
if only he had hidden in the forest –
even the witch's house would have done

The Search

Third Eye

who knows why she raises her hand imperiously
to protect the stone from the taint of another's touch
it lies there like an exotic creature as yet unnamed
its glint lingering in the almost absent light
her eyes dance over the deep purple
amethyst crystal spewed out of a Uruguayan volcano
she speaks with fire of its power to heal

once there were nights trapped in insomnia
the wind howling like a hungry devil
once there were days of a black sun
from an ominous galaxy and
her face contorted in the stained mirror

young British Bangladeshi woman
how omnipotent she is with her third eye
breathing the air of the heights
but some whisper
she's a Woman of the Occult
and rush away

The Search

A Small Jewess

the delicate fairy rises up
above the upturned faces
floats through glittering air
to an enchanted stratosphere
her white tulle skirt rising and falling
the men twirl her effortlessly
on her throne
she penetrates the shafts of light
reaches out to her beloved
he on another celestial throne
the men hold him poised
muscles hardened, faces sweating
the bride and bridegroom
stepped out of Vitebsk
whirl around to the rhythmic Jewish music
the groom's family smile tolerantly
the Jewish bride and her Christian bridegroom
in love but
in her speech, she claims she is just
A Small Jewess

*Vitebsk is the town in which Chagall grew up. He depicts his dreams of traditional
Jewish life there in many of his paintings.*

The Search

Open Ulcers

Melbourne to Sydney, an inch on the map
eleven hours the train jogged on a single track
sliced the wearisome landscape in two
Wangaratta, Wagga Wagga, Cootamundra, Wodonga
not station names I was accustomed to
Aboriginal names on scalloped roofed stations
just like the English ones used to be

there were no distant church spires
no hedgerows bursting with pink stars
no thatched cottages decorating winding lanes
only the heat that betrayed
that lay on the untouchable vastness
only the tiredness of parched grassland
of overbearing hills, of the sun's angry rays

I know that this land devours men
girls once disappeared into the dry hills
the open ulcers of the ancient continent
draw out tremors in Australians
sucked into the menace of landscape

so let's ride the train that haunts my mind
crashing through the forest of
billowing, twisting plants
convulsing trees, roots splayed upside down
thrusting their way up from the depths

Hotel Breakfast

at Shavuot
the hotel dances with delight
the guests breakfast by the dazzling sea
the roses breathe out fragrantly
beneath the virginal awning
fluttering in the caressing breeze
and the wine bottles stand poised
the loaves of hallah recline
ready for the blessings
and the black-robed rabbi
carefully undoes the cloth belt
round his slobbering belly
the better to devour
his breakfast plate layered
high with temptation.
And the families! Babies to grandparents
shouting, pinching cheeks, planting kisses
father is mother bird feeding her young ones
pops herring portions
into his toddler's waiting mouth.
And the laughing waiter!
he's high on joy
spins around the tables
rushes out glass jugs of lemonade
crammed with ice cubes, lemon slices, mint leaves

now the breakfast courtyard echoes
only the guests' shadows cling on
the settees and armchairs yawn at us
the silent corridors hardly remember
the footsteps, the running feet

and I recall
I saw a people
cast off their cocoon

Restaurant in Casablanca

the robe spins, undulating
whirls faster, faster
and settles, fluttering down
the whirling dervish

dimly lit restaurant
blue-robed circular table
faces animated
the woman says nothing
absorbs their words
'No Israelis in World Trade Centre
Israeli plot
crashing plane
metal distorted
into Star of David
Nazi aggression of Israelis
Arab lands
world domination
by American Jews.'
Endless talk
nodding heads

now is the moment
words chase around her brain
like a spinning top
struggle to escape
remain incarcerated
she sits mute
her mouth set tight
her lips sealed
as if sewn together

stares at her cold china plate
she longs to be invisible

she will be Persephone
Hades will surely reach up for her
carry her under his arm
she will disappear downwards
through a fissure in the restaurant floor
they must suspect
the strangeness of her silence
they talk on excitedly
oblivious of the voiceless woman
drenched in fear and shame
too afraid to blurt out
'I'm a Jew!'

the words spin round and round
the dervish reappears
and the cloth rises up
then words and cloth
twirl in a mad frenzy

April 2002

We Gotta Get Away

city of dreams, city of music
down south
on the Gulf of Mexico
trumpets, saxophones blared out
blues and jazz, day and night
crawfish, red beans
key lime tarts, chocolate snowballs
oh my!
the streetcars rattled
all along Canal Street

now the water stagnates
the stench sickens
the depths' hidden secrets
the corpses ignored
oil swirls on the surface
sordid debris floats
the wrath of Katrina
the power of the storm
the force of the water
as it rushed in

Hey please give us water, food, shelter
We gotta get away

the heat, unbearable
dehydrated, exhausted
miserable, powerless
they wave from rooftops
push the old in plastic boxes
sit dejectedly

heads in hands
in despair, they wait and wait
shout angrily
appeal between sobs

Hey please give us water, food, shelter
We gotta get away

the levees broke
the water surged in
oh New Orleans
suffering city
you people on the breadline
you poor, you hungry, you homeless
how many more deaths?
they are your people
Mr Bush

Hey please give them water, food, shelter
Get them away

The Walls

high above the city I am a tightrope walker
the difference is I dare not raise my head
if I stumble on the pitted stones I may tumble
so I step gingerly as if balancing on a thread

the sound of Arabic wafts up from a cafe
shutters crash down and are locked
plastic chairs are piled high for the night
the nargilas smokers have long fled

the Wall slithers slowly through history
a fairy-tale serpent with a glittering back
the fast dropping twilight whispers of fear
thin shadows lie in wait, I must make haste

there beckons a woman in embroidered robes
the moon rests on her electric white veil
I bear my blessing in a pomegranate flower
wary of the evil eye that may inflict its power

we wallow in silk cushions, sip mint tea from cut glasses
our words cannot speak, our eyes tell of concealed stories
Umm Kulthum sings on the radio, we dissolve in the music
the silver arched mirror guards the night it reflects

in shalah, may Jews and Arabs rejoice together
may they open their hearts as they did in past ages
it will come to pass in the fullness of days, after all
I carefully placed my wish in the Wailing Wall

The Wailing Wall is the last remaining wall of the Jerusalem Temple which was destroyed in 70 AD. It has become a place of pilgrimage for Jews to lament its loss and it is customary to place slips of paper containing written prayers and wishes into the crevices of the Wall.

Day Tripper

they are serene rolling hills
but they are not.
zones A, B and C are stamped on the landscape
without its permission
the despondent hills suffer in silence

Jerusalem sits high against a foreboding sky
its gates locked sternly against the refused
sad city that mourns those who may not enter
our guide may not venture in
prohibited.

Hebron is a town
but it is not.
H1 and H2 zones are superimposed on it
giant stilts stand over the streets
popping eyes magnify us

Palestine is an Escher print
walls, impossible, perpetual
fenced off roads, concrete barriers, checkpoints
trapped in the labyrinth
hands press against the walls

far from home the tourists' chatter ceases
Palestinian daughters bear platters of chicken and rice
their father's humiliation carved in his face
who is the bearded man in the photo on the wall?

the lament of life measured out by curfews
we who have spray-painted 'freedom' on the wall
we who go home
will speak of those half-lived lives

Rickety House

the wind sweeps across this morose land
dangerous forces shake the rickety house
now she hears the venom she cannot stand

ranting and roaring they are not banned
the hate trolls emerge and quickly pounce
and the wind sweeps across the land

their verdict is guilty and be damned
her vision in the cracked mirror screams and howls
as she hears the venom she cannot stand

in her body the wounding arrow brands
the hate trolls bang their drums, aroused
and the wind sweeps across the land

she'd dreamed of utopia, of a glorious land
she'd wear beads, adorn herself with flowers
But she hears the venom she cannot stand

now her resistance has been fanned
let the trial of the anti-Semites commence
still the wind sweeps across this land
still she hears the venom she cannot stand.

7th June 2016

The Search

Holy Arch

I walk through the holy arch
alarm goes off
they beckon me
security woman approaches
orders me: Arms out
stand in this machine
like the robot diagram
she swipes me with her sensor
it shrieks and cries
hungry, angry sensor
zaps me again, again
it's my bra I say
she brandishes the voracious sensor
remember Brussels, she hisses
glares at me darkly
it is forbidden to speak
but I am not a robot
I complain
security manager appears
threatens me with cubicle search
it is forbidden to speak
but I am not a terrorist!

Heavy Metal

door ajar
shaft of light imprisons toxic dust
silver ball revolves
reflects a mirror world
horizontal shadows on the floor
lipstick-stained shattered glasses
sunken imprints on red plush seats
oh mirror, mirror, what did you see?
and the echoes, the echoes of heavy metal
embedded in walls

forlorn winter leaves
spent roses shrouded in cellophane
blackened candle wicks on wet pavement
sodden photos, dribble of ink tears
and the air, the air spews drops of rain
cars splatter by in the grey drizzle

words fall out of mouths
hollow words
sanctimonious voices
now is the time for silence
and the silence, the silence flows over
the numb silence of wild stares, of sighs
and the mist, the ashen mist rises from the Seine

Second Generation

stepping softly I follow them
a sprightly lady, long dress swishing
strolls through a garden of dreams
tinted pink with blossom
two little girls each clutch a hand
a boy astride a bike
a threesome round a table in a summer house
all are smiling
I sidle up to them and
smile too

Summer 1999

traffic thunders along, lorries bound for Warsaw
the suffering street remembers its name changes
Kalischerstrasse, Hitlerstrasse, Stalinstrasse, ul.Adam Mickiewicz
A crumbling grey house
car park at the side, courtyard at the rear
I stand stock-still in the yard
washing dangles around me
curious people surround me
incomprehensible language

'My father lived here,' I say in German
so excited I can barely speak
the old man nods knowingly, turns to the others
they converse rapidly
incomprehensible language
they stare at me, tigers on the defensive
finally the old man says
'I remember your father

he came back to visit after the War.'

I am caught in the tangle of time
the lady, the girls, the boy, the threesome,
they are gone. I came too late.
Others live over their shadows.

Lower Silesia in Germany became Polish in 1945.

Singing Edith Piaf

it was the time of the trees opening their cloak of leaves
to wrap round and embrace the people
of melody clinging to the rusting canopy
of ochred parchment nonchalantly fluttering down
in the Luxembourg Gardens

it was the time of swaying and playing reverie
accordionist and violinist on the filigree bandstand
like a Robert Doisneau photo
and she sang and swayed too
Sous le ciel de Paris, S'envole une chanson

it was the time of linking arms in solidarity
of the *chansons* oozing from their youth
of madly spinning the *valse* in the Midi sun
of the nights in a café waiting for him
it was the time of red roses turning black

it was the time of May '68 and the barricades
the winding stairs she groped her way up
the *minuterie* that switched off too soon
the grimy wash basin on the landing
the darkened room
Sous le ciel de Paris

Pursuing Lost Time

on the old Prague Jewish Town Hall,
the clock hands follow the Hebrew letters
backwards round the clock
pursuing lost time

we always wander eastwards
down the hazy mists of time
clutching at pasts we never knew
searching for mythical family places

always to Jewish cemeteries
with dripping gravestones
the shock of destroyed graves
shiny villas lined up
where our dead had lain

once, face wan, hair flying
I wandered the streets of Berlin
searching for murdered relatives
only ghosts lurked in the pale winter
below the crying sky

in Holosov in Moravia
the synagogue casts its shadow over me
the wooden pews are empty now
a Catholic woman tells a story
her mother, the rabbi's family cook
sent food to them in Terezin

the daughter's voice breaks
she brushes away her tears

then our wounds swell
our scars rupture
memory chokes us

The Women's Hair

last night I dreamt of locks of long black hair
piled up to the ceiling in a concrete silo
some hung on butcher's hooks like horses' tails
they were all so dull and dusty and forlorn

they cut off the fertile tresses from your scalps
the stubble on your heads was coarse to the touch
weeping hair sent far across the sleeping ocean
now trapped in crates of locks turned white with shock

your hair was once as lustrous as the night sea
it shimmered deep burgundy and pearlised blue
your plaits hung down your dresses like silken ropes
and your Taipak hats perched jauntily
when the Uyghur rhythms set you dancing
your glistening braids spun madly
and away you flew

July 2020

The Search

Biography

Jennifer Langer

A long-time writer of poetry for herself, Jennifer's work has been published in various magazines and she is a member of an inspiring poets' collective.

Jennifer is editor of four anthologies of exiled literature: *The Bend in the Road: Refugees Writing* (1997), *Crossing the Border: Exiled Women's Writing* (2002), *The Silver Throat of the Moon: Writing in Exile* (2005) and *If Salt Has Memory: Contemporary Jewish Exiled Writing* (2008) all published by Five Leaves. She is lead editor of *Resistance: Voices of Exiled Writers* (Palewell, 2020).

She is founding director of Exiled Writers Ink which brings together established and developing migrant and refugee writers from repressive regimes and war-torn situations. Established in 2000, it is an ever-expanding organisation that provides a space for exiled writers to be heard, develops and promotes their creative literary expression, and crucially advocates human rights through literature and literary activism.

Previously co-editor of Exiled Ink magazine, she has written numerous articles on aspects of the literature of exile and has presented papers both in the UK and overseas, ranging from Casablanca to Gothenburg. She also reviews poetry, memoir, fiction and research focusing on migration, exile, memory and identity.

She holds a PhD from the School of Oriental and African Studies, University of London, in Cultural Memory and Literature by Exiled Iranian Jewish Women, and an MA in Cultural Memory from the School of Advanced Study, University of London. She is currently a SOAS Research Associate.

Jennifer is the daughter of refugees who escaped from Nazi Germany and who met in England. Her parents were both the sole survivors of their respective families.